MY FIRST LOOK AT COUNTRIES

A PICTURE OF MEXICO CITY IN MEXICO

Mexico

ADELE RICHARDSON

CREATIVE EDUCATION

Published by Creative Education

123 South Broad Street, Mankato, Minnesota 56001

Creative Education is an imprint of The Creative Company

Designed by Rita Marshall

Photographs by Getty Images (Nigel Atherton, Tom Bean, Chris Cheadle, Nick Dolding,

Richard During, Robert Frerck, George Grall, David Hiser, Suzanne Murphy, MATIAS

RECART / AFP, Luca Trovato)

Copyright © 2007 Creative Education

Printed in the United States of America

Library of Congress Cataloging-in-Publication Data

Richardson, Adele, 1966- Mexico / by Adele Richardson.

p. cm. — (My first look at countries)

Includes index.

ISBN- 13 : 978-1-58341-448-4

1. Mexico—Juvenile literature. I. Title.

F 1208,5.R5 2006   972—dc22   2005051776

First edition 9 8 7 6 5 4 3 2 1

Mexico

THE TRIANGLE-SHAPED COUNTRY

Mexico is a country south of the United States. South is below the United States on a map. Mexico is part of the **continent** called North America. Mexico is at the bottom of the continent.

Mexico is a long country. It is shaped like a triangle. Mexico is **bordered** by water on the left and right sides. It has lots of beaches!

Mexico is outlined in yellow on this map

Mexico is warm most of the time. It is even warm in the winter. Summer in Mexico can be very hot! Some parts of Mexico get lots of rain in the summer. Other places stay dry.

Wow! What a Land

Mexico has many kinds of land. There are lots of mountains in Mexico. Some of the mountains are very tall. In the south, or bottom, part of Mexico, there are **volcanoes**. **Lava** and ash sometimes come out of them.

Chewing gum is made
from a tree that grows in
the south part of Mexico.

ONE OF MEXICO'S TALLEST MOUNTAINS

There are many plateaus (*plah-TOWZ*) in the middle part of Mexico. Plateaus are high, flat areas of land. **Desert** covers the north, or top, part of Mexico. Few trees grow in the desert.

Some parts of Mexico are forests. Other parts are farms. Many farmers in Mexico grow wheat and beans. Some grow fruits such as bananas and pineapples.

The Pacific Ocean is on
one side of Mexico. The Gulf of
Mexico is on the other side.

CACTUSES GROW IN SOME OF MEXICO'S DESERTS

Cool Critters

Many kinds of animals live in Mexico. There are bears, deer, and wild sheep. Snakes and lizards live in Mexico, too. Lots of birds live in Mexico. Eagles live in the north. Colorful parrots live in the south.

Many animals live in the water near Mexico. Seals and dolphins live in some places. Whales swim near Mexico. Sea turtles come onto the beaches.

PRETTY MACAWS ARE AT HOME IN MEXICO

Monarch butterflies spend the winter in Mexico. They come from Canada and the United States. The butterflies fly to a forest in the middle of Mexico. They find the same trees every year! They fly north again in the spring.

MILLIONS OF MONARCHS FLY TO MEXICO EACH YEAR

COSTUMES IN MEXICO CAN BE BIG AND BRIGHT

People in Mexico have big fiestas on Independence Day. Independence Day is on September 16. People celebrate the day Mexico became a country. They have picnics. Parades move through the streets. It is a day of fun for everyone!

FIREWORKS ARE PART OF INDEPENDENCE DAY

Hands-on: Fiesta Fun

Mexico's flag is green, white, and red. You can use these colors to make a fiesta decoration.

What You Need

A paper plate
Green and red crayons
Tape
Scissors
Streamers (red, green, or white)

What You Do

1. Color the left side of the paper plate green. Color the right side red. Leave the middle white.
2. Have a grown-up help you cut the streamers. They can be as long or short as you like.
3. Tape the streamers around the paper plate.
4. Wave your fiesta decoration!

PEOPLE IN MEXICO TAKE PRIDE IN THEIR FLAG

Index

Words to Know

bordered—to have something at the edges; Mexico has water at its edges

continent—one of Earth's seven big pieces of land

desert—a dry, sandy area where few plants and trees grow

lava—hot, melted rock

volcanoes—mountains that hot rock, smoke, and ash come out of

Read More

Auch, Alison. *Welcome to Mexico*. Minneapolis: Compass Point Books, 2003.

Fontes, Justine and Ron. *Mexico*. New York: Children's Press, 2003.

Heiman, Sarah. *Mexico ABCs: A Book About the People and Places of Mexico*. Minneapolis: Picture Window Books, 2003.

Explore the Web

Mexico http://www.tooter4kids.com/Mexico/index.htm

Mexico For Kids http://www.elbalero.gob.mx/index_kids.html

Zoom School: Mexico http://www.enchantedlearning.com/school/Mexico